# Under the Sea

# Hermit Crabs
## and other
# Shallow-water Life

Sally Morgan

QEB Publishing

First published in the United States in 2008 by
QEB Publishing Inc.
3 Wrigley, Suite A
Irvine, CA 92618

www.qeb-publishing.com

Library of Congress Number: 2008010036

ISBN 978 1 59566 569 0

**Author** Sally Morgan
**Consultant** Camilla de la Bedoyere
**Editor** Sarah Eason
**Designed by** Calcium
**Picture Researcher** Maria Joannou

**Publisher** Steve Evans
**Creative Director** Zeta Davies

Printed and bound in United States

Picture credits
Key: T = top, B = bottom, C = center, L = left, R = right,
FC = front cover, BC = back cover

**Corbis** B Borrell Casals/Frank Lane Picture Agency 8,
Lawson Wood 11R, Tom Brakefield 16B
**Ecoscene** 15R, 18L, Phillip Colla 14–15,
Reinhard Dirscherl 10L
**Istockphoto** 20B, 21T
**Photolibrary** Anthony Bannister/Animals Animals 7T,
David B Fleetham/Pacific Stock 12–13, 13B, 17R,
F1 Online 18–19, Niall Benvie/Oxford Scientific 8–9,
Ralph A Clevenger/Flint Collection 4B, Randy Morse/
Animals Animals 14L, Reinhard Dirscherl/Mauritius 6B,
Richard Herrmann 19B
**Shutterstock** FC, 2–3, 3, 4–5, 5R, 6–7, 10–11, 12L, 16–17,
20–21, 22–23, 24

**Words in bold can be found in the glossary on page 22.**

# Contents

# Shallow-water homes

Areas where the land meets the sea are called coasts. Coasts change all the time. Waves crash onto them, shifting sand and breaking up rocks. Twice a day, the sea flows up to the **beach** and then falls away. These movements of the sea are called tides.

Kelp forests are found in coastal waters. They are homes to the animals that live there.

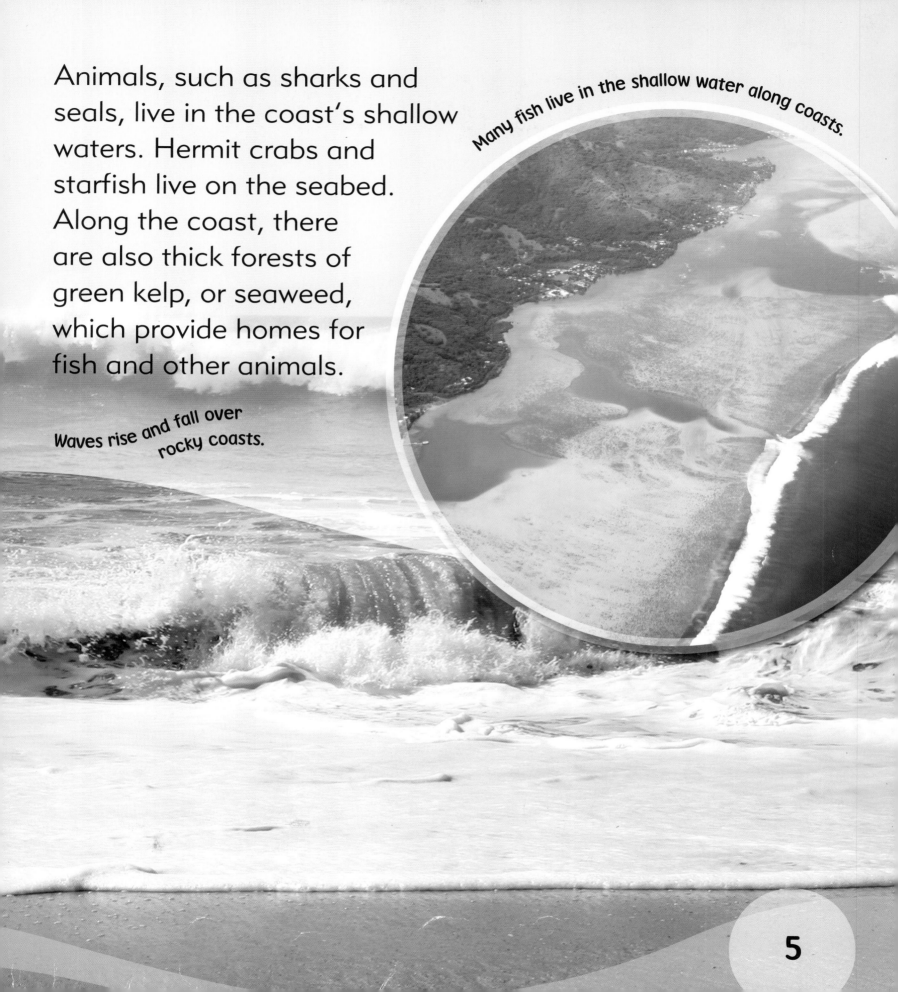

Animals, such as sharks and seals, live in the coast's shallow waters. Hermit crabs and starfish live on the seabed. Along the coast, there are also thick forests of green kelp, or seaweed, which provide homes for fish and other animals.

Many fish live in the shallow water along coasts.

Waves rise and fall over rocky coasts.

# Hermit crabs

Most crabs are protected by a hard shell, but the hermit crab has to borrow one from another animal. Instead of growing its own shell, the hermit crab pushes its soft body into an empty shell left by a sea snail.

Small animals called sea anemones attach themselves to the hermit crab's shell. They feed on the crab's leftover meals.

Sea anemone

Hermit crab

When the hermit crab grows bigger, it finds another empty shell that fits. It pulls its body out of the old shell and moves into a new one.

This hermit crab is looking for the perfect shell.

Hermit crabs have ten legs and two large eyes.

# Limpets

A limpet is a snail that lives on rocky shores and in kelp forests. It has a cone-shaped shell that looks like a pointed hat.

The limpet moves around using its large foot.

Foot

The limpet creeps over rocks in search of tiny plants called **algae** to eat. When the tide goes out, it returns to its favorite spot on the rock. It uses its strong **muscular** foot to cling onto the rock. It does not move until the tide comes in again.

Limpets can survive out of water for many hours if they are fixed to a rock.

9

# Starfish

The starfish is an **invertebrate**. An invertebrate is an animal that does not have a backbone. The starfish has at least five arms. Underneath the arms are tubelike feet with suckers. It uses the suckers to grip **prey**, such as **mussels**.

The starfish can use its strong feet to move pebbles.

Starfish pour the contents of their stomach over their prey to turn it into a mushy liquid. The starfish then sucks up the liquid.

Starfish can move at a speed of more than 3 feet (1 meter) a minute.

If a predator pulls off one of the starfish's arms, the arm will grow back.

11

# Octopuses

The octopus is an eight-armed animal. Each arm is covered with suckers that grip prey. The octopus uses its powerful **beak** to rip up and crush the prey into small pieces.

The octopus has two rows of suckers on each arm.

When an octopus is threatened, it releases a cloud of black ink into the water. This confuses the **predator**, so the octopus can slip away.

An octopus moves by crawling along the seabed using its arms. It can also swim very fast by pushing a jet of water out of its body at high speed.

The octopus' long arms are called tentacles.

The octopus squirts black ink from a tube inside its body.

13

# Garibaldi fish

The bright-orange garibaldi fish lives among the kelp off the coast of California. It lives alone, feeding on worms and crabs during the day and hiding in holes at night.

The male garibaldi fish guards its nest on the seabed.

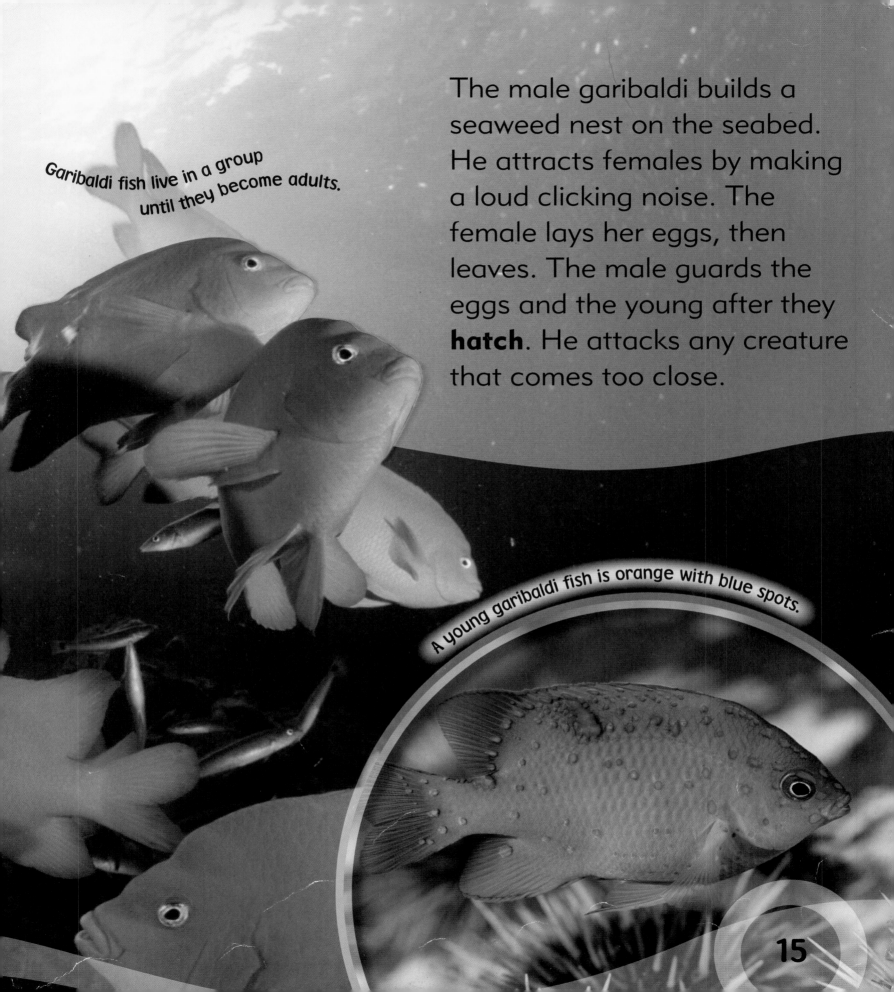

Garibaldi fish live in a group until they become adults.

The male garibaldi builds a seaweed nest on the seabed. He attracts females by making a loud clicking noise. The female lays her eggs, then leaves. The male guards the eggs and the young after they **hatch**. He attacks any creature that comes too close.

A young garibaldi fish is orange with blue spots.

# Eagle rays

The eagle ray has a pointed nose and a flattened body with huge winglike **fins**. It swims slowly through the water by flapping its wings. Occasionally, it leaps out of the water.

The mouth of the eagle ray is on the underside of its body.

Spotted eagle rays often swim in shallow water along sandy coasts.

mouth

Eagle rays search for food on the seabed.

The ray uses its strong teeth to crush the shells of seabed creatures, such as crabs and mussels. Its long tail ends in **poisonous spines**, which the ray uses to defend itself from attackers.

# Seals

Seals are **mammals**, but instead of legs, they have **flippers**. Their sleek, **streamlined** bodies make them expert swimmers.

Seals are clumsy on land, but very graceful in the water.

Like other mammals, seals have **lungs**, so they must come to the surface to breathe. However, seals can hold their breath for nearly an hour when they swim underwater.

Seals slowly wriggle onto land using their front flippers.

Seals use their front flippers to steady themselves when they are swimming slowly.

19

# Sea horses

The sea horse does not look like a fish. Its body is covered in armor-like scales and it uses its long tail to wrap itself around pieces of seaweed.

Some sea horses are disguised to look like bits of coral or seaweed.

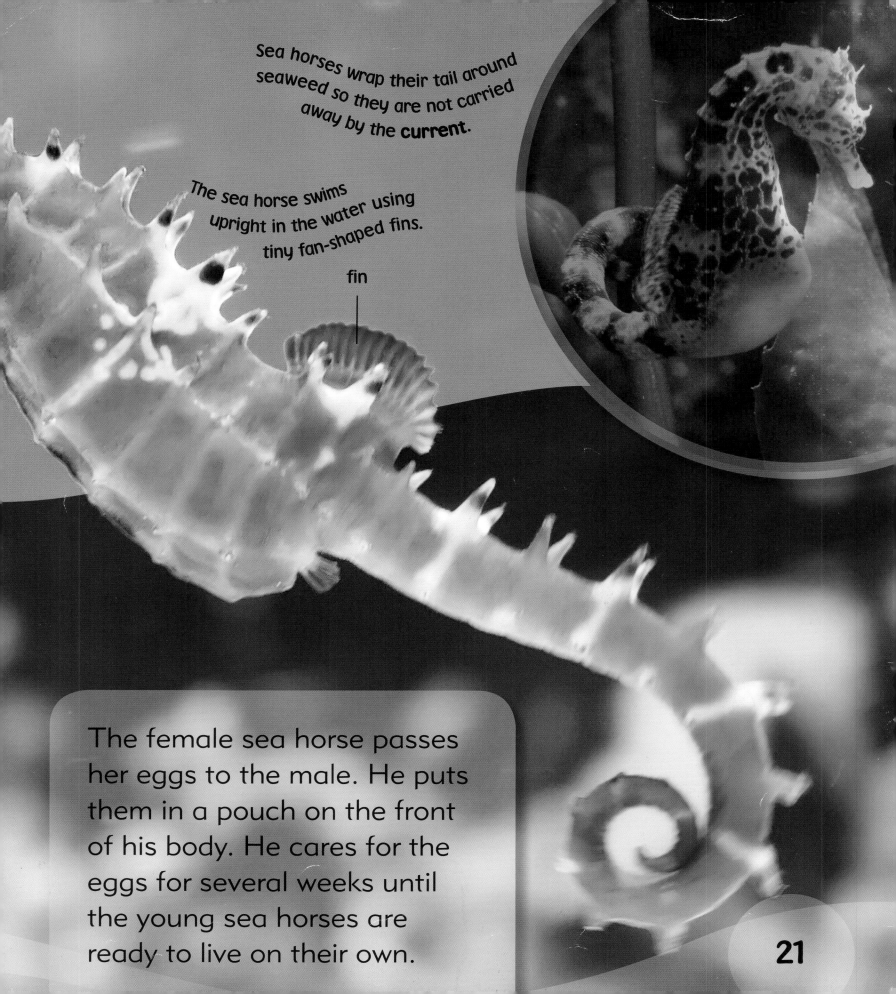

Sea horses wrap their tail around seaweed so they are not carried away by the **current**.

The sea horse swims upright in the water using tiny fan-shaped fins.

fin

The female sea horse passes her eggs to the male. He puts them in a pouch on the front of his body. He cares for the eggs for several weeks until the young sea horses are ready to live on their own.

# Glossary

**algae** tiny plants that are often eaten by sea animals

**beach** an area of sand where the sea meets the land

**beak** the hard snout used to catch prey

**current** the flow of water moving through the ocean

**fin** the part of a fish used to swim and steer

**flipper** a broad, flat limb of a mammal that lives in water

**hatch** when a baby animal breaks out of its shell

**invertebrate** an animal without a backbone

**lungs** the part of the body that an animal uses to breathe

**mammal** an animal that is covered with hair and gives birth to live young

**muscular** to have strong muscles

**mussel** sea creature with a soft body and hard shell

**poisonous spines** sharp parts of an animal's body that can hurt or kill another animal if touched

**predator** an animal that hunts other animals

**prey** an animal that is hunted by other animals

**streamlined** having a smooth shape that moves easily through water

# Index

# Ideas for teachers and parents

- Visit a rocky shore to go rock pooling. Make sure you visit when the tide is out, so you can see the rock pools. Look at the different animals, such as small fish, shrimps, and sea anemones. Lots of different snails live on the rocks. Take care when clambering across the rocks and keep a careful eye on the tide.

- Visit an aquarium to see the shallow-water creatures up close. Many aquariums have touch pools where children can see and touch animals, such as starfish and rays.

- Take part in a beach litter-pick. Lots of garbage is washed up onto beaches. Conservation organizations often run litter-picks on beaches where volunteers help to clean up the beach.

- Look for more information about rock pools in books and on the Internet. Encourage children to draw a rock pool and some of the animals that live there.

- Shallow waters and coasts are under threat from water pollution, over-fishing, and global warming. Find out more about these threats from books and the Internet.

- Encourage children to think up amusing stories and poems about the hermit crab and its life.

- Make a word search using the different ocean-related vocabulary in this book.